Informing the legislative debate since 1914

# Shipping U.S. Crude Oil by Water: Vessel Flag Requirements and Safety Issues

John Frittelli
Specialist in Transportation Policy

July 21, 2014

Congressional Research Service

7-5700

www.crs.gov

R43653

# Summary

New sources of crude oil from North Dakota, Texas, and western Canada have induced new routes for shipping crude oil to U.S. and Canadian refineries. While pipelines have traditionally been the preferred method of moving crude overland, they either are not available or have insufficient capacity to move all the crude from these locations. While rail has picked up some of this cargo, barges, and to a lesser extent tankers, also are moving increasing amounts of crude in domestic trade.

The rather sudden shift in transportation patterns raises concerns about the safety and efficiency of oil tankers and barges. The United States now imports less oil than five years ago by oceangoing tankers, while more oil is moving domestically by river and coastal barges. However, the Coast Guard still lacks a safety inspection regime for barges similar to that which has long existed for ships. The possibility of imposing an hours-of-service limit for barge crews as part of this regime is controversial. Congress called for a barge safety inspection regime a decade ago, but the related rulemaking is not complete. The Coast Guard's progress in revamping its Marine Safety Office is a related issue that Congress has examined in the past.

The majority of U.S. refineries are located near navigable waters to take advantage of economical waterborne transport for both import and export. However, for refineries switching from imported to domestic crude oil, the advantage diminishes considerably. This is because the Jones Act, a 1920 law that seeks to protect U.S. shipyards and U.S. merchant sailors in the interest of national defense, restricts domestic waterborne transport to U.S.-built and -crewed vessels. The purchase price of U.S.-built tankers is about four times the price of foreign-built tankers, and U.S. crewing costs are several times those of foreign-flag ships. The small number of U.S.-built tankers makes it difficult for shippers to charter tankers for a short period or even a single voyage, highly desirable in an oil market with shifting supply patterns. The unavailability of U.S.-built tankers may result in more oil moving by costlier, and possibly less safe, rail transport than otherwise would be the case. Some Texas oil is moving to refineries in eastern Canada, bypassing refineries in the northeastern United States, because shipping to Canada on foreign-flag vessels is much cheaper than shipping domestically on Jones Act-eligible ships.

Some of these issues may be addressed in the Coast Guard and Maritime Transportation Act of 2014 (H.R. 4005), which has passed the House, and the Coast Guard Authorization Act for Fiscal Years 2015 and 2016 (S. 2444), introduced in the Senate. The House bill requests federal agency studies and recommendations towards improving the competitiveness of the U.S.-flag industry while the Senate bill contains provisions related to oil spill response.

# Contents

# Figures

# Tables

# Contacts

# Introduction

New sources of crude oil from the Bakken region of North Dakota, the Eagle Ford and Permian basins in Texas, and western Canada have induced new routes for shipping crude oil to U.S. and Canadian refineries.[1] While pipelines have traditionally been the preferred method of moving crude overland, especially to or from landlocked locations, they either are not available or have insufficient capacity to move all the crude from these new sources of production.[2] Although much of this oil is now moving to refineries by rail,[3] waterborne transportation is playing an increasing role in moving crude oil within North America.[4] The quantity of oil moving by barge on the Mississippi River and its tributaries increased ten-fold from 2009 to 2013, and tanker shipments between the Gulf Coast and Atlantic Canada have grown at an even faster rate (**Figure 1**). There are no current data on the amount of domestic crude oil moving by barge or tanker to refineries along the Gulf Coast, but it is believed to have increased significantly since 2012.

**Figure 1. Waterborne Crude Oil Movements between Selected Regions**

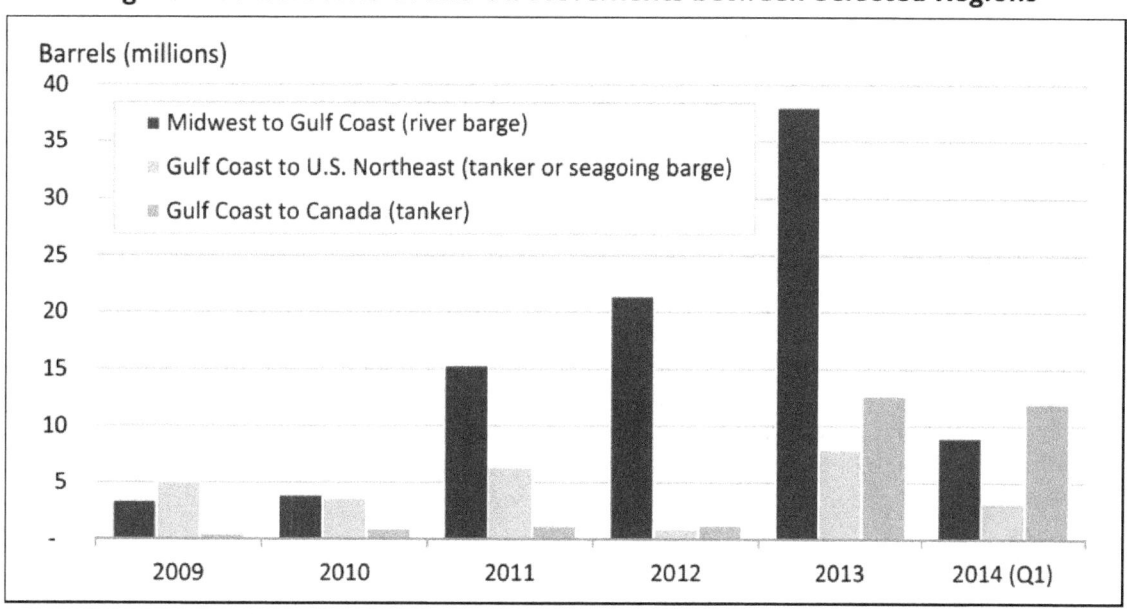

**Source:** U.S. Energy Information Administration,

Two aspects of the oil industry critically influence shipping patterns: (1) not all crude oil is the same and (2) each refinery is currently equipped to refine a certain blend of crude oils. Refineries in the Northeast are predominantly configured to handle crudes from the Bakken, Eagle Ford, and

---

[1] For further information on "unconventional" crude oil, see CRS Report R43148, *An Overview of Unconventional Oil and Natural Gas: Resources and Federal Actions*, by Michael Ratner and Mary Tiemann, and CRS Report R42032, *The Bakken Formation: Leading Unconventional Oil Development*, by Michael Ratner et al.

[2] For further analysis on the role of pipelines in moving crude oil, see CRS Report R41668, *Keystone XL Pipeline Project: Key Issues*, by Paul W. Parfomak et al.

[3] See CRS Report R43390, *U.S. Rail Transportation of Crude Oil: Background and Issues for Congress*, by John Frittelli et al.

[4] In this report, barge refers to both a river and a seagoing barge; tanker refers to a deep-draft, self-propelled ocean-going ship; and "tank vessel" refers to both a barge and a tanker.

---

Permian regions, but cannot efficiently refine oil sands crude from western Canada. There is greater variety in the capabilities of refineries on the Gulf and West Coasts. Reconfiguring a refinery to handle a different type of crude is possible but may be costly. The feasibility of doing so depends on the relative costs of various types of crude, the projected availability of the various crude oils, and the price spread between crude oil and refined petroleum products such as gasoline and diesel fuel.[5]

The sudden shift toward domestic sourcing of crude oil raises issues regarding the safety and efficiency of the maritime component of this new supply chain. These fall into two main categories. One concerns the Coast Guard's role in preventing oil spills by regulating the safety of vessels and the training and working conditions of crews.[6] The other has to do with the impact of the Jones Act, a 1920 law that restricts domestic waterborne transport to vessels built in the United States and crewed by U.S. citizens, which may now be affecting U.S. producers' decisions about how to ship crude oil and whether to send it to refineries in the United States or in Canada.

# New Shipping Routes

The vast majority of U.S. refineries are located along the coast (including the Great Lakes) or an inland waterway. Most coastal refineries traditionally have been supplied by imported crude, and some lack pipeline connections and may not be equipped or have the space to receive crude by rail. For this reason, large amounts of oil are being moved out of production areas by truck or rail, but are being transferred to barges or tanker ships for the last leg of the trip to a refinery.

Crude oil produced at Eagle Ford, TX, is conveniently located for waterborne transport due to its proximity to the coast. Some of it moves through the port of Corpus Christi, where outbound crude oil shipments nearly trebled from 2012 to 2013.[7] The nearby port of Victoria, TX, has also experienced a dramatic increase in crude oil barge traffic. It appears that most of the Texas crude moving by vessel goes to coastal refineries in Texas and Louisiana or to the Louisiana Offshore Oil Port (LOOP), an offshore ship-to-pipeline transfer facility. A comparatively small amount of Eagle Ford crude oil moves by water to refineries in proximity to New York Harbor and the Delaware River, but much larger quantities seem to be going to refiners in Canada's Atlantic provinces.

While much of the oil coming from the Bakken region moves to refineries by rail, there are now several well-established intermodal routes involving water transport. These include:[8]

- rail to barge at St. Louis and Hayti, MO, and Osceola, AR, on the Mississippi River, to Gulf refineries;

- rail to barge at Hennepin, IL, on the Illinois Waterway, to Gulf refineries;

---

[5] These factors are discussed in CRS Report R41478, *The U.S. Oil Refining Industry: Background in Changing Markets and Fuel Policies*, by Anthony Andrews et al.

[6] This report focuses on the Coast Guard's role in oil spill prevention. Regarding the agency's role in oil spill response, see CRS Report RL33705, *Oil Spills in U.S. Coastal Waters: Background and Governance*, by Jonathan L. Ramseur.

[7] http://www.portofcorpuschristi.com/index.php/general-information-155/statistics/monthly-reports.

[8] For further information on these and other routes, see BB&T Capital Markets, "Examining the Crude by Barge Opportunity," June 10, 2013.

- rail to vessel at Albany, NY, on the Hudson River, to East Coast refineries;

- rail to Yorktown, VA, for coastal transport to East Coast refineries;

- rail to vessel at Anacortes and Vancouver, WA, for coastal transport to West Coast refineries.

Pipeline to barge transfer is occurring at Cushing, OK, from where barges move the oil down the Arkansas and Mississippi Rivers to Gulf Coast refineries.

# Vessel Types and Capacities

New waterborne services moving crude oil from the Bakken or Texas generally do so with smaller vessels than the trans-oceanic tankers used to carry Alaskan and imported oil. The fleet can be divided into two broad categories: "brownwater" vessels operating on inland and near-shore waters and "bluewater" vessels operating in the open ocean.

A river barge can hold 10,000 to 30,000 barrels of oil.[9] Two to three river barges are typically tied together in a single tow, and thus a river tow of tank barges could carry 20,000 to 90,000 barrels. In addition to inland rivers, this type of barge configuration is used on the intracoastal waterway (an inland canal) along the coasts of Texas and Louisiana. River barges have speeds of about 4 to 5 miles per hour (mph).

A coastal tank barge designed for open seas (an articulated tug-barge, or ATB)[10] can hold 50,000 to 185,000 barrels. However, newer ATBs can carry 240,000 to 340,000 barrels, a capacity comparable to that of coastal tankers. Seagoing barges have speeds of about 10 knots (12 mph).

In contrast to coastal tank barges, a river barge can be used in "drop and swap" operation—that is, the tugboat can drop a loaded barge at a facility where it can be used for storing product while the tugboat is free to make other barge movements—so that the relatively expensive self-propelled portion of the vessel is not tied up while unloading, as a tank ship would be. The tugs designed for ATBs sail poorly without the barge, so they seldom perform drop and swap operations.[11]

A coastal tank ship can hold 300,000 to 650,000 barrels. The coastal tankers that are being deployed to move Texas crude carry 330,000 barrels and are referred to as "handysize" or "medium range" tankers. Coastal tankers have speeds of about 12-15 knots.

For comparison, tankers moving Alaska oil to the West Coast carry between 800,000 and 1.3 million barrels of oil and fall into the "Aframax" or "Suezmax" size categories. Very large or ultra-large crude carriers (VLCCs and ULCCs) that carry imported oil from overseas hold 2 to 3 million barrels. A crude oil pipeline moves between 400,000 and 800,000 barrels per day, enough to service the largest U.S. refineries. The unit trains[12] that move Bakken and Texas crude oil can carry 70,000 to 80,000 barrels. **Table 1** summarizes conveyances for moving domestic crude oil.

---

[9] A barrel of oil is equal to 42 gallons.

[10] The bow of the tug fits into a notch in the stern of the barge and the tug is hinged to the barge on both sides of its hull, allowing fore and aft (pitch) movement, such as over sea swells.

[11] George H. Reid, *Primer of Towing*, 3rd ed. (Centreville, MD: Cornell Maritime Press, 2004), p. 22.

[12] A unit train consists of only a single type of car, in this case crude oil tank cars, and is not broken up or reconfigured (continued...)

**Table 1. U.S. Crude Oil Conveyances**

| Conveyance | Capacity (000 barrels) | Cruising Speed | Crew Size | Inventory | Operating Geography |
|---|---|---|---|---|---|
| River barge | 20-90 | 4-5 mph | 4-10 | 3,500-4,000* | inland rivers, intracoastal waterway |
| Seagoing barge (ATB) | 50-300 | 10 knots (12 mph) | 6-12 | 86* | coastal U.S. |
| Handysize product tanker | 300 | 12-15 knots (14-18 mph) | 21-28 | 31* | coastal U.S. |
| Aframax or Suezmax crude oil tanker | 800-1,300 | 12-15 knots (14-18 mph) | 21-28 | 11*<br>1,400 (foreign-flag) | Alaska to Puget Sound and California, U.S. Gulf Coast to Eastern Canada |
| 100-car unit train | 70-80 | 40-50 mph | 2 | 45,000 crude oil tank cars/450 unit trains** | continental U.S., predominantly west-east |
| Crude oil pipeline | 400-800 | 3-8 mph | 1-2 (remote monitors) | 57,500 miles | predominantly midcontinent, south-north, Alaska |

**Source:** U.S. Department of Transportation; Army Corps of Engineers; Clarkson Research Services Ltd. *Tanker Register.*

**Notes:** *For domestic service, vessels must be U.S. built and U.S. flagged. **Tank car inventory increasing rapidly.

As **Table 1** indicates, the Jones Act-eligible fleet of crude oil tankers consists of 11 ships, all employed in moving Alaska crude oil to the U.S. West Coast or to a refinery in Alaska. Of the 86 seagoing barges, 42 can carry more than 130,000 barrels. While a tanker's capacity is better matched to the daily consumption rates of a single refinery than the capacity of a unit train or most barges, the limited fleet of Jones Act-eligible tankers has required some refineries with direct ocean access to ship domestic oil by barge or train or to continue to rely on foreign sources.

Jones Act-qualified ATBs and product tankers are also used to lighter ocean-going crude oil tankers.[13] Although it is technically feasible to do so, tank vessels do not readily alternate between carrying dirty oil (crude oil, residual fuel oil, asphalt) and refined (clean) petroleum products because the tanks would have to be extensively washed after carrying dirty product, a time-consuming and costly process. However, due to the recent increase in domestic crude oil production, particularly at Eagle Ford, some tonnage has shifted from the "clean" products trade to the crude oil trade.[14] Tankers that used to carry refined product from the Gulf Coast to Florida

---

(...continued)

between origin and destination.

[13] Lightering is the process of unloading a portion of an ocean-going tanker's load offshore, or at a harbor's entrance, to reduce the draft of the ship.

[14] Product tankers that carry chemicals are called parcel tankers, and since they have many more and smaller individual holding tanks than petroleum tankers, they would not be practicable for carrying petroleum.

(via the Port of Tampa) are now carrying crude oil because they can earn higher returns.[15] Barges are replacing them to move refined products to Florida, a development that has been blamed for higher gasoline prices in Florida.[16]

The decline of oil imports from overseas may free up some of the lightering fleet for the domestic crude trade. If West Coast refineries source more crude from the Bakken or Canada rather than Alaska, this could also free up Jones Act tankers. One such tanker is believed to have been redeployed to move crude oil from the Gulf of Mexico to the West Coast via the Panama Canal.[17] However, there is a limit to how many clean product tankers will switch to carrying crude oil. The crude oil boom has also led to a boom in U.S. refinery output, so there is also strong demand for clean product tankers.

## Vessel Size Relates to Voyage Distance

The most economic tank vessel size to deploy depends largely on voyage distance. The longer the voyage, the more incentive there is to use a larger vessel because of economies of scale at sea. The first VLCCs were built when the Suez Canal was closed in the late 1960s and tankers headed from the Persian Gulf to Europe and North America had to sail longer routes around South Africa.

Larger tankers face diseconomies of scale in port: they take longer to load and unload than smaller ships, and some port charges are based on vessel size. Thus, smaller vessels are used for shorter voyages, on which a tanker will spend a greater portion of its total time in port. Aframax and Suezmax tankers, considered of medium size, are being used to ship Alaska oil from Valdez to Seattle, a distance of 1,200 nautical miles, and to Los Angeles, a distance of 2,000 nautical miles. Similar tankers carry Texas oil to eastern Canadian refineries with sailing distances ranging from 2,300 to 3,000 nautical miles.[18]

Evidence from these other trades suggests that Aframax or Suezmax tankers would be the preferred vessels for shipments from Texas ports to Delaware River and New York Harbor oil terminals, a distance of 1,900 to 2,000 nautical miles, if such tankers were available in the Jones Act-eligible fleet. The handysize tankers that are now used for this purpose may be smaller than the preferred size. Prior to carrying crude oil, these handysize tankers were moving refined product on much shorter *intra*coastal voyages, such as from Houston to Tampa. From 2001 to 2011 (before the Texas and Bakken oil boom began) the average haul of Jones Act handysize product tankers was roughly 1,000 nautical miles while the average haul for the larger Jones Act Aframax and Suezmax crude oil tankers was roughly 1,700 nautical miles.[19]

ATBs are used on much shorter coastal voyages. From 2001 to 2011, their average haul was about 420 nautical miles (the approximate sailing distance between Norfolk, VA, and Charleston, SC). Since they are somewhat slower than tankers, on longer voyages they could require an additional

---

[15] "Shale Oil Has Revolutionized U.S. flagged Oil Tanker Fleet," *Petroleumworld.com*, July 1, 2013.

[16] The News Press, "Supply Shortage Fuels Gas Price Jump," November 21, 2013. According to the article, 97% of Florida's fuel is transported by vessel. The EIA also discusses the tight supply of vessels for transporting Florida's fuel; see, "The Spring Break Travel Rush and Changes in Florida's Gasoline Supply," *This Week in Petroleum*, March 26, 2014.

[17] Washington Analysis, LLC, *Energy Update: Alaska Oil Exports and Jones Act Tankers*, February 27, 2014.

[18] Tankers were identified with assistance from the U.S. Maritime Administration.

[19] U.S. Maritime Administration, *Coastal Tank Vessel Market Snapshot, 2011*, June 2012, p. 2.

day or two to reach destination. However, newer ATBs, which can be larger and faster, tend to be deployed on longer voyages. In 2010, coastal tank barges that were less than 10 years old accounted for 63% of overall coastal barge shipments less than 500 miles but 70% of the shipments 500 miles or more.[20]

# Maritime Safety Issues

The large increase in domestic waterborne shipment of crude oil and refined products comes at a time when the Coast Guard is reevaluating its regulations and industry oversight. Several new regulations are pending.

## New Barge Safety Regime

Barges are the workhorses in moving Bakken and Texas oil by water. However, the Coast Guard has just begun establishing a safety inspection regime for barges.

In the Coast Guard and Maritime Transportation Act of 2004 (P.L. 108-293, §415), Congress directed the Coast Guard to establish a barge safety inspection and certification regime similar to that which exists for ships. This includes establishing structural standards for vessels as well as standards for the crew. This new inspection regime will be more significant for tank barges used on rivers than for seagoing barges, because seagoing barges moving oil or other hazardous material are already inspected.[21] However, one pending rule would also apply to seagoing barges. Section 409 of the 2004 act authorized the Coast Guard to evaluate an hours-of-service limit for crews on towing vessels. This was in line with a 1999 National Transportation Safety Board (NTSB) recommendation that the Coast Guard establish scientifically based hours-of-service regulations for domestic vessel operators.[22]

On August 11, 2011, the Coast Guard issued a notice of proposed rulemaking on barge inspections and work hours.[23] In the notice, the Coast Guard states that on a schedule providing six hours of work followed by six hours of rest, as is typical on barges engaged in multi-day voyages, sleep debt accumulates and gradually increases crew members' fatigue levels.[24] ATB operators have filed comments opposed to addressing hours of service as part of this rulemaking, while maritime unions have filed comments in favor of a mandatory eight-hour rest period.[25] The NTSB filed comments reiterating its support of an eight-hour rest period. The Coast Guard has not issued final regulations.

---

[20] Ibid., p. 6.

[21] As per 46 U.S.C. subchapter I. River tows are subject to other regulations in Titles 33 and 46, C.F.R.

[22] NTSB, Recommendation M-99-1. The NTSB is an independent federal agency that investigates accidents in all modes of transportation and makes recommendations on how to improve safety.

[23] 76 *Federal Register* 49976-50050.

[24] See 76 *Federal Register* 49991-49997, August 11, 2011. Crews of towing vessels on the Great Lakes presently use a three-watch system as per 46 U.S.C. §8104(c).

[25] See http://www.regulations.gov, docket no. USCG-2006-24412.

# Crewing Requirements of ATBs vs. Tankers

According to an original designer of the ATB, "The American coastwise shipping business has grown in a way that differs from many other nations. The high cost of manning and building ships has led over the years to a coastwise transportation network dominated by tugs and barges."[26] ATBs are sometimes referred to as "rule breakers" within the maritime industry because they operate with smaller crews.[27] The Coast Guard determines crewing requirements based on the registered tonnage of a vessel, which for barges includes only the tug, not the barges the tug may be pushing. As a result, the crew required aboard an ATB is one-third to one-half the number required aboard a tank ship; an ATB typically has a crew of 6 to 12, versus 21 to 28 for a tank ship. (The precise number for each vessel type depends on the amount of automation.)

The Coast Guard's pending decision on hours of service could force ATBs to carry larger crews, possibly negating their economic advantage compared to tankers. This occurred previously with a precursor to the ATB called the integrated tug barge: when the Coast Guard increased their manning requirements in 1981, integrated tug barges lost their economic advantage, and none have been built since.[28] The Coast Guard increased manning requirements because integrated tug barges operated essentially as ships since the tug and barge seldom separated. While ATBs are designed for easier separation of tug and barge, as noted earlier, they also seldom separate.

The distinction in crewing requirements between ships and ATBs has been criticized for distorting the domestic shipping market by encouraging the use of otherwise less efficient (and perhaps less militarily useful) barges instead of ships.[29] A counterargument is that the problem is not the small crew size on ATBs but the excessive manning requirements for coastal tankers.

## Pace of Rulemaking an Issue for Congress

Congress has been concerned with the pace at which the Coast Guard is issuing barge safety regulations under the 2004 law. In the Coast Guard Authorization Act of 2010 (P.L. 111-281, §701), Congress requested that all rulemakings related to oil pollution prevention, including barge inspection, be finalized within 18 months of enactment (i.e., by April 15, 2012). The 2010 act (§702) also required the Coast Guard to promulgate additional regulations to reduce the risk of oil spills in operations involving the transfer of oil from or to a tank vessel. The Coast Guard has issued a request for public comments, but has not yet proposed regulations.[30]

---

[26] Robert P. Hill, Ocean Tug & Barge Engineering, "The Articulated Tug/Barge – ATB: The History and State of the Art," http://www.oceantugbarge.com/PDF/history.pdf.

[27] See, Jeff Cowan, "The Articulated Tug Barge (ATB) Quandary," February 13, 2013; Robert P. Hill, "Responding to "The Articulated Tug Barge Quandary," April 5, 2013; and Tom Allegretti, "Safe Operation, Proven Results," April 17, 2013, all at http://www.MarineLink.com.

[28] Navigation Vessel Inspection Circular (NVIC)-2-81, February 25, 1981.

[29] IHS Global Insight, *An Evaluation of Maritime Policy in Meeting the Commercial and Security Needs of the United States*, January 7, 2009, p. 37.

[30] See 78 *Federal Register* 63235, October 23, 2013.

# Performance of the Coast Guard's Marine Safety Office

The Coast Guard's ability to provide effective safety oversight of certain maritime operations has been a long-standing concern. In response to questions raised by Congress in 2007,[31] the Coast Guard acknowledged that its practice of regularly rotating staff geographically or by activity, as military organizations typically do, was hindering its ability to develop a cadre of staff with sufficient technical expertise in marine safety.[32] In response, the agency created additional civilian safety positions, converted military positions into civilian ones, and developed a long-term career path for civilian safety inspectors and investigators.[33] Despite these changes, at an October 2011 meeting to discuss inspection regulations towing operators complained about having to rehash the same issues with a "revolving door" of Coast Guard officials.[34] They also asserted that the Coast Guard was placing too much emphasis on a one-day-per-year inspection of vessels and equipment and not enough emphasis on human factors, the leading cause of marine accidents.

The number and quality of the Coast Guard's investigations and reports of marine accidents, as well as the lack of a "near-miss" reporting system, have been noted by the Department of Homeland Security Inspector General (IG) and other observers as missed opportunities to learn from past incidents. A May 2013 IG audit concluded:[35]

> The USCG does not have adequate processes to investigate, take corrective actions, and enforce Federal regulations related to the reporting of marine accidents. These conditions exist because the USCG has not developed and retained sufficient personnel, established a complete process with dedicated resources to address corrective actions, and provided adequate training to personnel on enforcement of marine accident reporting. As a result, the USCG may be delayed in identifying the causes of accidents; initiating corrective actions; and providing the findings and lessons learned to mariners, the public, and other government entities. These conditions may also delay the development of new standards, which could prevent future accidents.

The IG found that at the 11 sites it visited, two-thirds of accident inspectors and investigators did not meet the Coast Guard's own qualification standards. The IG noted that the shortage of qualified personnel would be further compounded by the new towing vessel safety regime, which would expand the inspections workload. In response to this audit, the Coast Guard stated it was developing a "Maritime Prevention Enhancement Plan" that it hoped to complete in FY2014. In the Coast Guard Authorization Act of 2010 (P.L. 111-281, §521), Congress requested an annual report from the Coast Guard assessing the adequacy of its marine safety workforce.[36]

---

[31] House Committee on Transportation and Infrastructure, Subcommittee on Coast Guard and Maritime Transportation, Hearing on Challenges Facing the Coast Guard's Marine Safety Program, July 27, 2007.

[32] See the 2007 report on the Coast Guard's marine safety mission by a retired Coast Guard vice admiral at http://www.uscg mil/hq/cg5/cg54/docs/VADM%20Card%20Report.pdf.

[33] U.S. Coast Guard, "Enhancing the Coast Guard's Marine Safety Program," September 25, 2007; http://www.uscg mil/marinesafetyprogram/. See also *Coast Guard Proceedings*, Summer 2008, pp. 20-28, available at http://www.uscg mil/proceedings.

[34] http://www regulations.gov/#!documentDetail;D=USCG-2006-24412-0095.

[35] DHS, Office of Inspector General, "Marine Accident Reporting, Investigations, and Enforcement in the U.S. Coast Guard," OIG-13-92, May 2013; http://www.oig.dhs.gov/assets/Mgmt/2013/OIG_13-92_May13.pdf.

[36] This report has been delivered to Congress; http://www.uscg mil/hq/cg8/cg82/.

# The Jones Act

The Jones Act requires that vessels transporting cargo between two U.S. points be built in the United States, crewed by U.S. citizens, and at least 75% owned by U.S. citizens.[37] The law was enacted in 1920 (Merchant Marine Act of 1920, §27, P.L. 66-261).[38] One of the motivations for the U.S.-build requirement was to facilitate the disposal of cargo ships constructed during World War I by the U.S. Shipping Board, a government agency set up in 1916 to purchase, construct, and operate merchant ships during the war. The Jones Act authorized the sale of these vessels to the private sector.[39]

The Jones Act stated an explicit national policy of supporting a U.S. merchant marine and a U.S. shipbuilding industry in the interest of national defense. That policy remains in the law today:[40]

> It is necessary for the national defense and the development of the domestic and foreign commerce of the United States that the United States have a merchant marine (1) sufficient to carry the waterborne domestic commerce and a substantial part of the waterborne export and import foreign commerce of the United States and to provide shipping service essential for maintaining the flow of waterborne domestic and foreign commerce at all times; (2) capable of serving as a naval and military auxiliary in time of war or national emergency; (3) owned and operated as vessels of the United States by citizens of the United States; (4) composed of the best-equipped, safest, and most suitable types of vessels constructed in the United States and manned with a trained and efficient citizen personnel; and (5) supplemented by efficient facilities for building and repairing vessels.

Because of the restrictions on shipbuilding and crewing, Jones Act ships tend to be more costly to build and operate than vessels used by foreign-flag ocean carriers, which can order vessels from whichever shipyards offer the lowest bids and typically hire most of their crew members from countries where seafarers' wages are much lower than in the United States.

## Jones Act Shipping Rates

According to oil shippers, the price for moving crude oil from the Gulf Coast to the U.S. Northeast on Jones Act tankers is $5 to $6 per barrel, while moving it to eastern Canada on foreign-flag tankers is $2.[41] For a Texas oil producer using a tanker with capacity of 300,000 barrels, this rate difference amounts to receiving $1 million less for a shipment of oil to a U.S. refinery than for a shipment to a more distant Canadian refinery. In consequence, from January

---

[37] The law is codified at Title 46 U.S.C. Chapter 121, Documentation of Vessels (46 U.S.C. §§12101-12152) and Title 46 U.S.C. Chapter 551, Coastwise Trade (46 U.S.C. §§55101-55121).

[38] The Act was named after Senator Wesley L. Jones, Washington State, Chairman of the Senate Interstate and Foreign Commerce Committee, who also included a provision to ensure that trade between Alaska and the lower 48 states not be shipped through Vancouver, Canada (to the benefit of Seattle).

[39] The ships were sold for about one-tenth the cost of construction. They had high-speed engines and other features that were useful for military operation, but that made them relatively costly to operate in commercial service.

[40] 46 U.S.C. §50101.

[41] *Bloomberg Businessweek*, "U.S. Law Restricting Foreign Ships Leads to Higher Gas Prices," December 12, 2013; *Platts Oilgram News*, "Regulation and Environment," September 9, 2013. See also Senate Committee on Energy and Natural Resources, Testimony of Faisel Khan, Managing Director, Integrated Oil and Gas Research, Citigroup. Hearing to Explore the Effects of Ongoing Changes in Domestic Oil Production, Refining and Distribution on U.S. Gasoline and Fuel Prices, July 16, 2013.

2013 through March 2014, more than twice as much Gulf Coast crude oil was shipped by water to Canada as was shipped to U.S. Northeast refineries.

Refineries in the U.S. Northeast consumed about 12 times as much crude oil from fields offshore of eastern Canada as oil shipped from the Gulf Coast in all of 2013. They also consumed imports from Nigeria, Saudi Arabia, and other countries. Shipping rates for these imports, regardless of country of origin, are much lower than domestic shipping rates for Gulf Coast oil (**Table 2**).[42] (Shipping oil from the Gulf Coast to eastern Canada costs more than shipping it from Africa to the U.S. Northeast because ice-class tankers must be used to serve Canadian refineries for a portion of the year.)

### Table 2. Ocean Shipping Rates to U.S. Northeast Refineries

Dollars per barrel

| Origin | Estimated Rate |
|---|---|
| U.S. Gulf Coast | $5.00-$6.00 |
| Eastern Canada | $1.20 |
| Nigeria | $1.45-$1.70 |
| Saudi Arabia | $1.90 |

**Source:** *Platts Oilgram News*, "Regulation and Environment," September 9, 2013; *Platts OilGram Price Report*, McGraw Hill Financial, January-April, 2014.

Although there is currently no Bakken oil moving from Washington or Oregon ports to California refineries, the cost aboard a Jones Act tanker is estimated to be $4 to $5 per barrel; as the oil would have to move from the Bakken region to the ports by rail at a cost of about $9 per barrel, the total shipping cost would be $13 to $14 per barrel. The cost of shipping Eagle Ford oil through the Panama Canal to these refineries is estimated to be $10 per barrel.[43] By comparison, shipping oil from Ecuador to West Coast refineries costs around $3.25 per barrel, and Iraqi oil about $2.30 per barrel.[44]

Jones Act rates for shipping Alaska oil to West Coast refineries are not available, but Bakken oil shipped by rail to Pacific Northwest refineries is beginning to displace Alaskan oil. Alaska oil producers could look to resume exports to Asia to replace lost shipments to the U.S. West Coast. However, as specified by Congress when it lifted the export ban on Alaska North Slope oil in 1995 (P.L. 104-58), the oil must be exported on U.S.-crewed and -flagged tankers, although the tankers do not need to be U.S. built. After the Alaska export ban was lifted, roughly 5%-7% of Alaskan oil was exported, mostly to South Korea, Japan, and China, but exports ceased in 2000.[45]

In the case of crude oil, the price coastal refineries are willing to pay is based on the international price of oil, as a refinery has no way to raise the prices of gasoline and other refined products if

---

[42] *OilGram Price Report*, McGraw Hill Financial, January-April, 2014.

[43] En*Vantage, Inc., "The Surge in US Crude Oil Production," Presentation to PFAA 20th Annual Conference, October 24, 2013; http://www.pfaa-online.com/docs/2013/AC/8EnVantage-PFAA-Oil-Presentation-102413.pdf.; Bloomberg, "Texas Vies with Saudi Arabian Oil in California Shipments," January 29, 2014.

[44] *OilGram Price Report*, McGraw Hill Financial, January-April 2014 reports.

[45] U.S. Energy Information Administration, Petroleum and Other Liquids, Imports/Exports and Movements, http://www.eia.gov/petroleum/data.cfm#imports.

its transportation costs are higher than those of its competitors. In order to minimize transportation costs, U.S. oil shippers have favored barges over ships for coastwise transport, but this may have reduced the shipment distances over which domestic waterborne oil is price competitive. The long-term decline in the amount of petroleum carried domestically by tankers is reflected in the diminished capacity of the privately owned Jones Act-eligible tanker fleet (see **Figure 2**). Following World War II, the relatively small U.S.-flag tankers in international service were gradually replaced by much larger foreign-built tankers. Many of the Jones Act-eligible tankers in domestic service were replaced by tank barges following enactment of a double-hull requirement for tank vessels in the Oil Pollution Act of 1990. The decline of oil production in Alaska, which has fallen by about 46% over the last decade, also contributed to reduced demand for Jones Act-eligible crude oil tankers, causing some to be scrapped.

## Figure 2. U.S.-Flag Privately-Owned Tanker Fleet

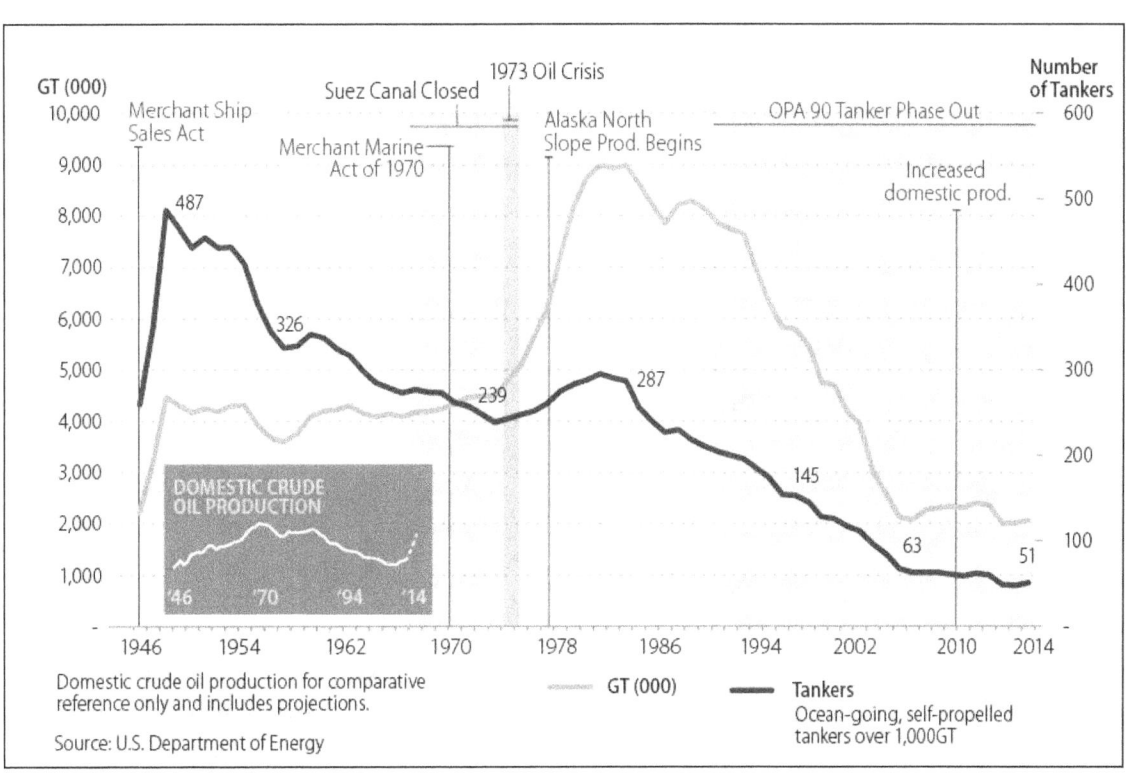

**Source:** CRS modification of figure from U.S. Maritime Administration.

**Notes:** GT= gross tonnage, an indication of the cargo capacity of a ship. Figures pertain to both Jones Act (domestic) and international tankers.

## Domestic Tanker Construction Costs

According to data from the U.S. Maritime Administration (MARAD), an agency of the U.S. Department of Transportation, and from industry sources, the cost of domestically built tankers is approximately four times the cost of tankers of similar size built in foreign shipyards (**Table 3**). Almost all oceangoing tankers are built in Asia; in 2012, Korean shipyards received 60% of worldwide orders for new tankers, Chinese yards 30%, and Japanese yards 8% (measured by ship capacity). U.S. shipyards' prices are higher even though major ship components, like the engines, are built in foreign yards. The purchase price of new river tugs and barges in the United States is not considered to be as great a deterrent to river transport, perhaps because barges are simpler to build and are ordered in sufficient quantities that shipyards can achieve some economies of scale.[46]

As **Table 3** indicates, tank ships are more expensive to build than ATBs. They require more scantling (interior framing) and more freeboard (the height of the hull from the water to the deck) than barges. However, tank ships have significant advantages over barges. They can operate in more adverse weather conditions than ATBs, are faster, and have superior fuel economy. The U.S. Energy Information Administration estimated in 2012 that the cost of moving crude oil from the Gulf Coast to Northeast refineries by tanker would be about half the cost of moving it by barge—not counting the cost of construction.[47] This suggests that tankers could have a competitive advantage over barges on longer coastal voyages if domestic shipbuilding costs were lower or if foreign-built tankers could be employed.

### Table 3. U.S. and World Prices for Tanker Vessels

(Cost of a newbuild, based on recent deliveries or construction contract announcements)

| Vessel Type | Capacity | U.S. Price | World Price |
|---|---|---|---|
| Handysize product tanker (aka medium-range tanker) | 40,000-50,000 dwt 330,000 bbl | $100-$135 million | $30-$35 million |
| Ocean-going ATB (smaller) | 27,000 dwt 185,000 bbl | $60-$85 million | not available |
| Ocean-going ATB (larger) | 45,000 dwt 250,000-300,000 bbl | $100-$130 million | not available |
| Aframax tanker | 80,000-120,000 dwt 650,000-800,000 bbl | $200 million | $45-$55 million |
| Suezmax tanker | 130,000-160,000 dwt 1 million bbl | No recent builds | $55-$65 million |
| Very Large Crude Carrier (VLCC) | 200,000-320,000 dwt 2 million bbl | No recent builds | $90-$100 million |

**Source:** U.S. Maritime Administration, Title XI Ship Financing Guarantees, Pending and Approved Loan Applications; American Petroleum Tankers S-1 SEC Filing; RBN Energy LLC; RS Platou Economic Research, annual and monthly reports; press releases from Kinder Morgan, Teekay Tankers, Scorpio Tankers, Euronav; Poten and Partners, *Weekly Tanker Opinion*.

The Tariff Act of 1930 (19 U.S.C. §1466), requires that U.S.-flag ships pay a 50% *ad valorem* duty on any non-emergency repairs conducted in foreign shipyards. A 2011 MARAD study[48] of

---

[46] U.S. shipyards have recently been able to export offshore supply vessels (servicing offshore oil platforms), indicating more competitiveness in this category of vessels as well.

[47] U.S. Energy Information Administration, "Additional Information on Jones Act Vessels' Potential Role in Northeast Refinery Closures," May 11, 2012.

[48] U.S. Maritime Administration, *Comparison of U.S. and Foreign-Flag Operating Costs*, September 2011.

ships operating in international trade found that ship repair costs for U.S.-flag ships are 1.3 times those of foreign-flag ships. The MARAD study found that many U.S. ships have repairs performed in foreign yards because, even with the 50% duty, the total cost is less than if the repairs were performed in a U.S. domestic shipyard.

# U.S.-Flag Vessel Operating Costs

A 2011 MARAD study comparing U.S.-flag versus foreign-flag operating costs in international trade found that U.S.-flag vessels' operating costs were substantially higher—2.7 times higher. (This higher operating cost does not reflect higher domestic construction costs, because U.S.-flag ships engaging in international trade do not have to be built in the United States.) The study estimated the average daily operating cost of a foreign-flag ship to be under $6,000.[49] A separate MARAD study in June 2012 estimated the daily operating cost of a Jones Act tanker to be $22,000, which would be about 3.7 times the operating cost of a foreign-flag tanker. A major reason U.S.-flag vessels cost more to operate is that they are crewed by U.S. citizens. The crews on most foreign-flag ships are drawn mainly from poor countries and are paid significantly less than U.S. merchant seafarers.

According to MARAD, the daily operating cost of an ATB ($13,000) is almost half that of a U.S.-flag tanker ($22,000).[50] Since an ATB might travel two to three knots slower than a tanker, it might require additional sailing time. On a voyage from Texas to New York, an ATB would require two additional sailing days, reducing the ATB's cost savings over a tanker to about one-quarter, assuming that the vessels carry similar amounts of oil. However, only five ATBs in the Jones Act fleet match the capacity of a handysize tanker (330,000 barrels). Most ATBs now in use carry half as much oil as a tanker, thus requiring two voyages to match the capacity of a tanker; their operating cost per barrel of oil on this comparatively long voyage is likely to be higher than that of a tanker. A large tanker carrying oil from Nigeria to the U.S. East Coast, requiring two weeks sailing time, would be expected to have lower overall operating costs and lower operating costs per barrel than a U.S.-flag tanker ship or ATB making the much shorter domestic voyage.

## The Missing Triangle Trade

One consequence of the relatively high cost of building and operating Jones Act tankers is that they cannot compete effectively for international cargo. This results in Jones Act tankers sailing empty much of the time, further raising shipowners' costs.

A key aspect to improving the economic competitiveness of freight carriers is reducing empty travel miles. If Jones Act product tankers were price competitive in the international market, they could triangulate their trade routes, perhaps moving diesel fuel from Gulf Coast refineries to Europe, then carrying European gasoline to the U.S. Atlantic Coast before sailing in ballast (carrying only ballast water for stability) to the Gulf Coast to repeat.[51] In this triangular route, two out of three voyages would generate revenue and the ballast sailing distance would amount to 18% of the total sailing distance. With their costs rendering them uncompetitive on international routes, however, Jones Act product tankers typically sail "piston" routes, carrying crude oil or

---

[49] U.S. Maritime Administration, *Comparison of U.S. and Foreign-Flag Operating Costs*, September 2011.

[50] U.S. Maritime Administration, *Coastal Tank Vessel Market Snapshot, 2011*, June 2012, p. 6.

[51] Michael D. Tusiani, *The Petroleum Shipping Industry* (Tulsa, OK: PennWell, 1996).

refined products from the Gulf Coast to the East Coast and then returning in ballast, thus earning revenue on only half the trip.

A peculiar triangular trade has developed to circumvent the Jones Act requirements. This involves Gulf Coast refineries shipping gasoline to the Bahamas, where additives are mixed in before the product is moved to the U.S. Northeast. So long as the product is processed in the Bahamas, both water movements can be made in foreign-flag tankers.[52] The savings from using foreign-flag shipping are apparently greater than the cost of an additional tanker unloading and loading operation.

## Chartering and the Jones Act

Because of the Jones Act, U.S. oil shippers also cannot take advantage of the current surplus in the world tanker fleet, caused in part by the drop-off in crude oil shipments to the United States. If it were accessible, chartering could be done on a spot basis (for a single voyage) or on a time basis (for six months to two years). Given the rapid changes in the U.S. oil market, some shippers might prefer the flexibility of chartering to the long-term financial commitment required to build a pipeline or a rail terminal. However, the number of Jones Act-qualified tankers is small, and most appear to be tied up in charters lasting several years. Current Jones Act charter rates are $75,000 to $100,000 per day, up from about $50,000 per day in the 2010 through 2012 period.[53] In the world market, charter rates for tankers of similar size ("medium range") have fluctuated around $10,000 per day for spot charters and $15,000 per day for 12-month time charters.[54]

A spot market is also valuable because it lowers the overall cost of moving oil for everyone by adding fluidity to tanker supply. For instance, the sailing times of tankers cannot always be synchronized exactly with loading schedules. If an oil company's tanker is two weeks early for a shipment, rather than idling its tanker for that time, the company can re-let the tanker in the spot market for someone else's use. The oil company could then charter someone else's tanker for its intended shipment. In other words, by pooling the tanker supply in the spot market, the fleet is used more efficiently. By segregating the domestic shipping market from the international market, the Jones Act undermines a competitive advantage of tankers against pipelines, namely their status as mobile assets that can be redeployed in response to market changes.

## Waterborne vs. Pipeline

Before the advent of oil produced from shale deposits and its movement by rail, tank vessels and pipelines were the primary options for moving oil. Both modes can move crude oil to refineries in lot sizes of hundreds of thousands of barrels, fitting a large refinery's daily intake needs. Economies of scale are important to both, but installing a larger pipe reduces the transportation cost per barrel more rapidly for pipelines than building a larger vessel does for ship lines. For this reason, oil companies typically share use of a large pipeline rather than building smaller individual pipelines. Pipelines face a disadvantage in that they must acquire, build, maintain, and pay property taxes on their rights of way, not only for the pipe but also for the pumping stations, whereas navigation infrastructure in harbors (shipping channels) and on inland waterways (locks

---

[52] Reuters, "Customs About-face Could Make Bahamas Key Source For U.S. Gasoline," April 23, 2014.

[53] RBN Energy LLC, "Rock The Boat – Don't Rock The Boat – The Jones Act Coastal Trade," January 12, 2014.

[54] RS Platou Economic Research, Monthly Report – May 2014; http://www.platou.com/dnn_site/Default.aspx

---

and dams) is largely provided by the federal government. As indicated in **Table 1**, pipelines move product between 3 and 8 mph, so tankers have a speed advantage. This can be important when oil prices are volatile. On the other hand, pipelines are extremely dependable in delivering product on time, so little safety stock is needed.

## Economies of Scale Diverge

Over recent decades, pipeline operators have managed to ship more oil with less pipe. Pipeline mileage leveled off in the 1980s. Since then, miles of trunk line have actually decreased but capacity has increased because the pipes are larger in diameter.[55] The amount of oil carried per mile of trunk line pipe is about 37% higher today than it was in the 1980s.

In contrast, Jones Act carriers are utilizing smaller, rather than larger, vessels to transport oil, a result of increasingly relying on barges rather than tankers in coastwise transport. In 1980, barges represented 39% of the total cargo capacity of the tank vessel fleet (barges and tankers).[56] In 2012, barges accounted for 82% of the total cargo capacity and carried about 65% of the coastwise refined product tonnage. The shift from tankers to barges is significant, because what should be the least-cost method for transporting crude oil and petroleum products is being utilized less than it might be in favor of a method that is cost-competitive due only to regulation.

The divergence in economies of scale between the pipeline and waterborne modes parallels a trend in their respective modal shares. In 1979, pipelines handled 58% of crude oil shipments (measured in ton-miles)[57] and waterborne carriers 41%. For refined products, 44% moved by pipeline and 48% by water. By 2009, pipelines were carrying 80% of crude oil shipments to 19% for ships and barges, and 63% of refined products movements went by pipeline as opposed to 26% by water.[58] Part of the reason for the change in modal share in refined product was a sharp decline in use of residual fuel oil for heat and power, which affected waterborne market share.[59] Today, tanker ships are used in domestic trade primarily where there is no pipeline service, as with crude oil shipments from Alaska to the lower 48 states and gasoline shipments from the Gulf Coast to Florida.

Pipelines appear to be preferred over river transport as well. Pipelines are used heavily to move Gulf Coast crude oil north to the Upper Midwest, carrying about 30 million barrels a month, whereas barges do not carry any crude oil upriver on the Mississippi waterway system. Barges have less than 10% of the market for refined products moving between the Gulf Coast and the Upper Midwest.

---

[55] Pipeline statistics are available from *Oil and Gas Journal*.

[56] U.S. Army Corps of Engineers, Navigation Data Center; http://www.navigationdatacenter.us/.

[57] A ton-mile is one ton of freight moved one mile.

[58] Association of Oil Pipelines, *Shifts in Petroleum Transportation*, data reproduced by the Bureau of Transportation Statistics, *National Transportation Statistics*, Table 1-61; http://www.rita.dot.gov/bts/sites/rita.dot.gov.bts/files/publications/national_transportation_statistics/html/table_01_61.h tml.

[59] Federal Trade Commission, Bureau of Economics, *The Petroleum Industry: Mergers, Structural Change, and Antitrust Enforcement*, August 2004, p. 210. A potential decline in the use of heating oil in New England, in favor of natural gas, similarly might affect waterborne and pipeline share in the future because much of the heating oil is carried by barge from New York Harbor.

**Waterborne vs. Pipeline for Coastal Transport of Refined Products**

Since production of refined products is more geographically dispersed than it is for crude oil, the competition between tanker and pipeline for moving refined products is more prevalent. A shift in relative costs between the two modes can change modal shares significantly, as happened in the early 1960s when the Colonial Pipeline was built.

By far the highest volume domestic route for shipping U.S. petroleum liquids is from the Gulf Coast to the Northeast. The U.S. government built two pipelines along the East Coast during World War II after German submarines sank 48 U.S. coastal tankers in four months. After the war, the pipelines were sold to private interests, and one was converted to natural gas. Despite the pipeline, the route continued to be the most important for U.S.-flag product tankers.

In the summer of 1961, U.S. seafarers staged an 18-day strike which idled 114 ships on the Gulf to East Coast run. It ended with a federal injunction, but with issues mostly unsettled. U.S. seafarers achieved higher wages but no success against using foreign-flag tankers to import oil. In 1962, nine oil companies announced plans to build a 22" to 36" pipeline from Houston to New York Harbor to move 600,000 barrels a day of refined product. The oil companies cited maritime strike disruptions and higher seafarer wages, along with new pipeline technology allowing for larger-diameter pipe, as reasons why the pipeline would be more economical than ships. The maritime industry estimated the pipeline would take one-third of its cargo and reduce fleet size by 50 tankers. The need for the pipeline depended upon continuation of federal restrictions on the amount of oil that could be imported. It was believed that if the import restrictions were lifted, the pipeline might not be built because the foreign-flag supertankers then coming into use could deliver foreign oil and refined products to the U.S. Northeast more cheaply than the pipeline could bring refined products from Texas. The Colonial Pipeline was completed in 1963. Automation was then increased aboard Jones Act tankers to reduce crew sizes and improve ships' competitiveness against the pipeline. At about the same time, three maritime strikes on the West Coast induced plans for a West Coast refined products pipeline. In 1965, a pipeline was completed from Puget Sound refineries to Portland, OR.

Today, the Gulf Coast ships approximately 75 million barrels per month of refined products to East Coast states by pipeline. About 15 million barrels per month move to East Coast states by tanker or barge, mostly to Florida, which receives no pipeline service. The East Coast imports about 30 million barrels per month of refined products, about a third from Canada and the rest from Europe, Nigeria, and Venezuela. Meanwhile, the Gulf Coast exports 75 million to 100 million barrels per month of refined products.

On the West Coast, Oregon receives 90% of its refined product from refineries in Puget Sound via pipeline and some from California by vessel. The Gulf Coast ships less than 5 million barrels per month of refined products to California by pipeline and nothing by vessel (via the Panama Canal). Although California is the third-largest state in terms of refining capacity, it also imports a substantial portion of its refined product needs, mostly from the Pacific Rim, Mexico, and Africa.

## Waterborne vs. Railroad Options

For the many refineries located on the coasts, the cost of rail versus vessel transport is particularly relevant. Phillips 66 has chartered two Jones Act product tankers to move crude oil from Eagle Ford, TX, to its Bayway refinery in Linden, NJ (in proximity to New York harbor). The company also supplies that refinery with Bakken oil via railroad (or rail to barge via the Port of Albany), as well as with imported oil from West Africa.[60] The refinery has a capacity of 238,000 barrels per day.

Rail and coastal transport are competitors in supplying crude oil to the coastal refineries that process similar types of crude. Vessels, especially tankers, have superior economics in moving crude, which is why so many refineries are located on the water. A 330,000-barrel tank ship can move the equivalent of four to five unit trains of oil. A larger tanker, of the size used in the Alaska

---

[60] Phillips 66, Earnings Conference Call, October 30, 2013, Q&A.

trade, can move the equivalent of 15 unit trains. With the median capacity for U.S. refineries of about 160,000 barrels per day, even the smallest tankers can carry a two-day supply of oil. Rail loading and unloading terminals are being built to accommodate four to five trains per day to match a refinery's delivery needs; the challenge has been developing high-speed pumping equipment that can load/unload an entire train (100 to 120 tank cars) in sufficient time to avoid train backups at terminals (a unit train is over a mile long). On the other hand, coastal refineries already have docks and pumping facilities to receive vessels. Moreover, railroads must build and maintain track and pay property taxes on their rights of way, whereas the cost of building and maintaining navigation channels in harbors is largely born by the federal government. For these reasons, tanker should be significantly cheaper than rail for transport of crude oil, even when the water route is much longer.

A round-trip voyage from the Gulf to the Northeast might take two weeks. Thus, to sustain a supply chain for one refinery, a fleet of several tankers would be needed. As Jones Act-eligible tankers are in very short supply, however, refineries such as Bayway utilize waterborne transport as a supplement to the more expensive rail option from the Bakken. Phillips 66 has stated that if Jones Act eligible tankers were available, it would run 100,000 barrels a day of Gulf Coast oil to this refinery.[61] In 2013, an average of 22,000 barrels a day of Gulf Coast oil was shipped to all seven U.S. Northeast refineries.[62] By rail, Bayway alone receives 50,000 barrels per day and is completing a rail terminal with capacity to unload 75,000 barrels a day.

Eagle Ford crude oil is not currently shipped to California refineries, but such shipments are estimated to cost $14.50 per barrel.[63] The estimated cost of shipping Eagle Ford oil in Jones Act tankers to California through the Panama Canal is $10 per barrel. Again, the water route is cheaper than rail even though the railroad route is only one-fourth the length of the water route. The Panama Canal route would also be cheaper than moving Bakken oil to California refineries via rail to the Pacific Northwest followed by coastwise vessel transport to California, with a total cost of $13 to $14 per barrel.[64] When the Panama Canal's expansion project is completed in 2015, tankers with capacity of 600,000 barrels will be able to pass through, twice the size of the largest tankers using the canal today. This would further increase the cost advantage of ocean transport, if Jones Act-eligible vessels of that size are available.[65]

---

[61] Phillips 66 presentation at Bank of America Merrill Lynch Refining Conference, March 6, 2014.

[62] According to EIA, *Crude Oil Movements by Tanker and Barge between PADD Districts*; http://www.eia.gov/dnav/pet/hist/LeafHandler.ashx?n=PET&s=MCRMTP1P31&f=M.

[63] En*Vantage, Inc., "The Surge in US Crude Oil Production," Presentation to PFAA 20th Annual Conference, October 24, 2013; http://www.pfaa-online.com/docs/2013/AC/8EnVantage-PFAA-Oil-Presentation-102413.pdf

[64] En*Vantage, Inc., "The Surge in US Crude Oil Production," Presentation to PFAA 20th Annual Conference, October 24, 2013; http://www.pfaa-online.com/docs/2013/AC/8EnVantage-PFAA-Oil-Presentation-102413.pdf.

[65] When Alaskan oil began flowing in 1977, West Coast refineries could not handle all the oil. The excess was shipped from Valdez, AK, to Panama on supertankers and transferred there to smaller tankers that could fit through the canal's locks en route to Gulf and East Coast. The high cost of this shipping route ($4 to $5.25 per barrel) led to calls for allowing exports of Alaskan oil to Japan and Korea (with shipping costs of $0.60 per barrel). Later, a pipeline was built across Panama to replace the vessel transit through the Canal.

# Figure 3. Selected Water and Rail Crude Oil Supply Routes

(Freight rates per barrel)

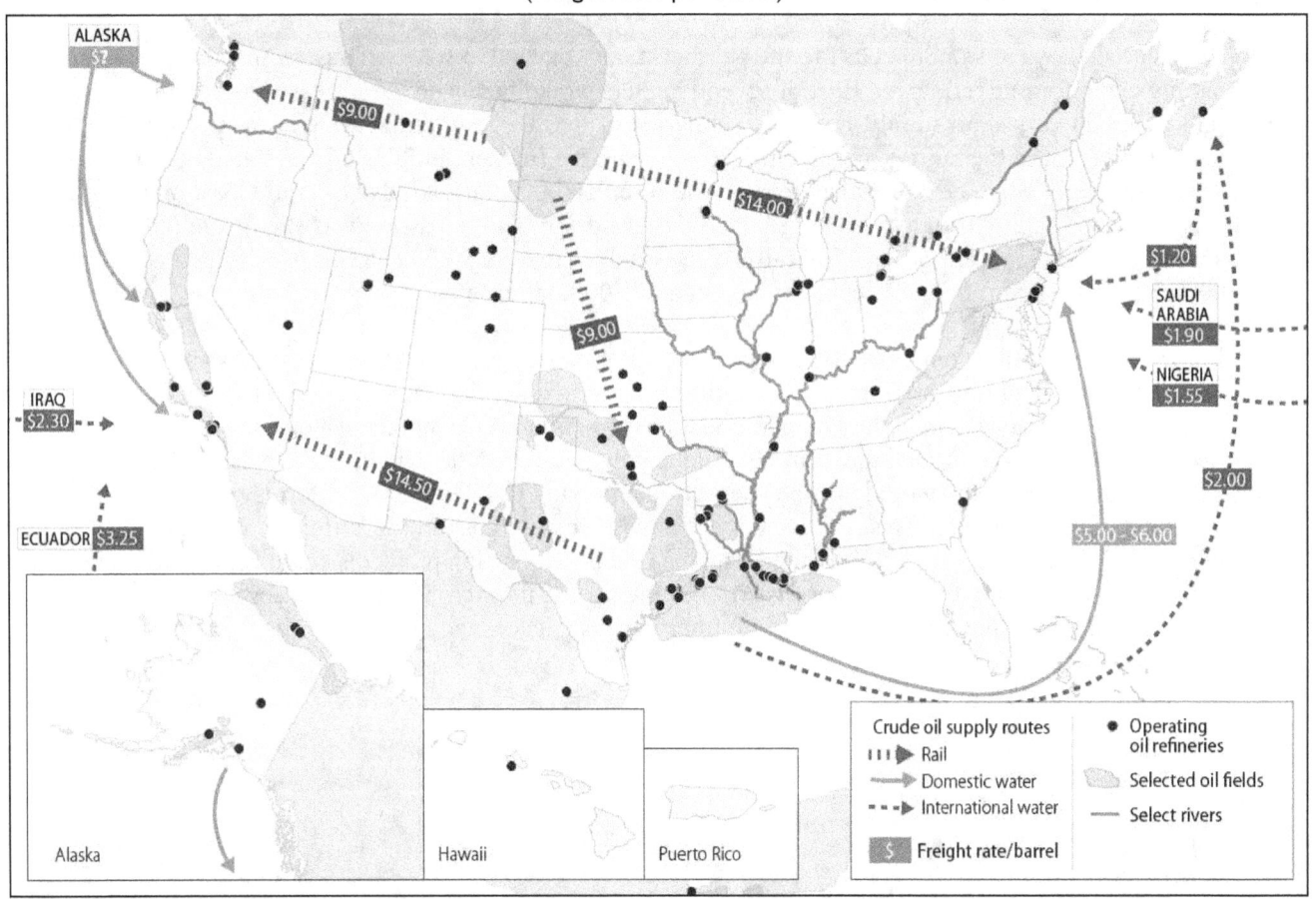

**Source:** Graphic created by CRS. Map boundaries and information generated using HSIP Gold 2013 – For Official Use Only (Platts); Esri Data & Maps (2013 Census (2013). Shipping rates approximated from those reported by Turner, Mason & Co. in Platts *Oilgram Price Report*, January-April 2014 issues, and as foo text.

It is not inconceivable that tankers could also play a role in moving Bakken oil to East or West Coast refineries, although the route would be circuitous compared to rail. Significant amounts of Bakken oil are moved to Gulf Coast terminals by a combination of pipeline, railroad, and barge for refining within that region. From a Gulf Coast port, tankers could transport the oil either to East or West Coast refineries. Existing rail and pipeline connections serve Great Lakes ports, from which tankers could move Bakken oil to Northeast refineries. The experience of agricultural producers in the upper Midwest, however, suggests that these two routing options are not economically feasible because of the Jones Act.[66]

Notwithstanding the U.S.-flag requirement for Alaska oil exports, the situation is somewhat similar to that of Texas oil in that higher domestic shipping rates encourage sales to foreign buyers. This shipping pattern is not unique to oil. In the 1960s and 1970s, the U.S. lumber industry in Washington and Oregon asserted that the Jones Act hindered its ability to compete with western Canadian lumber that could be shipped at cheaper international freight rates to the U.S. east coast. Today, Oregon and Washington are still large waterborne shippers of forest products, but all their products shipped by water are exported while all the forest products the East Coast receives by vessel are imported.[67] Other bulk shippers have made similar assertions.[68]

## Waterborne Transport and Concerns about Rail Safety

If Eagle Ford, and possibly Bakken oil producers were able to access foreign-flag tankers at international rates of around $2 or perhaps less per barrel, some of their domestic oil shipments would likely shift from rail to water.[69] That shift could be beneficial in terms of the safety of oil transport, although the allowance of foreign-flag tankers could potentially displace U.S. seafarer jobs.

Congress is greatly concerned about the safety of shipping crude oil by rail. Existing railroad tank cars are inadequately designed to prevent release of product during derailment, and the transportation of crude oil in unit trains, a new development, has meant that a single incident can involve a large quantity of flammable and explosive material. Incidents involving unit trains of crude oil have caused numerous fires and explosions, requiring evacuations and in one case resulting in 47 fatalities.[70] Railroads have increased track and equipment inspections on oil routes, and have reduced the speeds of unit trains of crude oil through populated areas. However, recent incidents have shown that a high proportion of derailed tank cars will puncture and release

---

[66] Grain and feed producers in the upper Midwest contend that while they can move product economically by barge to New Orleans or by rail to a Great Lakes port, from there, because of the Jones Act, they have no economical access to dry bulk ships that could deliver the feed to eastern North Carolina hog and poultry farms. These farms import their feed from Canada and South America, See, for instance, "Can Soybeans Compete?" *Top Producer*, Spring 2005.

[67] U.S. Army Corps of Engineers, Navigation Data Center, http://www navigationdatacenter.us/wcsc/wcsc htm.

[68] These include grain and feed, scrap metal, and road salt producers. See U.S. Congress, House Committee on Transportation and Infrastructure, Subcommittee on Coast Guard and Maritime Transportation, *The Impact of U.S. Coastwise Trade Laws on the Transportation System in the United States*, 104th Cong., 2nd sess., 1996, 104-66.

[69] See, for example, the comments of the CEO of Phillips 66 during the company's earnings conference call, July 31, 2013.

[70] For details, see CRS Report R43390, *U.S. Rail Transportation of Crude Oil: Background and Issues for Congress*, by John Frittelli et al.

---

product even at much lower speeds. The capability and resources of local responders to crude-by-rail incidents are ongoing concerns.[71]

In contrast, tankers are not a new method for moving oil. Vessels have double hulls and vessel operators are required to have emergency response equipment and resources in place in case of a spill. The Coast Guard has a regulatory regime in place to safeguard tanker transits through harbors. Where allowed, states have imposed additional safeguards on tankers transiting their harbors. Environmental damage from an oil spill remains a grave concern, but tanker incidents generally do not require evacuations of towns and cities.

## Impact on Other Rail Users

The heavy reliance on railroads to move crude oil has interfered with the smooth functioning of the rail system. This has had negative consequences for other rail users, including passengers as well as freight shippers.

From 2008 to 2013, annual rail car loadings of crude oil increased from 9,500 to over 400,000. In 2014, railroads are expected to move 650,000 tank cars of crude oil, the equivalent of 18 unit trains of 100 cars per day.[72] Many of these shipments move out of the Bakken region of North Dakota, and grain, sugar beet, potato, and coal shippers have complained of serious delays in rail service in the Upper Midwest.[73] Amtrak cancelled several trains across North Dakota because the freight railroad that owns the track could not accommodate them, and on other occasions it has had to substitute bus service between points in North Dakota for rail service.[74] Based on past experience, local rail backups can have ramifications for service nationwide.

Some railroads are installing new track to handle the growing demand to ship oil by rail. If tankers were available and their operating costs more competitive with rail costs, it is possible that increased use of waterborne transport could relieve some of the pressure on rail service.[75]

---

[71] U.S. Congress, House Committee on Transportation and Infrastructure, Subcommittee on Railroads, Pipelines, and Hazardous Materials, Oversight of Passenger and Freight Rail Safety, 113th Cong., 2nd sess., February 26, 2014; U.S. Congress, Senate Committee on Commerce, Science, and Transportation, Subcommittee on Surface Transportation and Merchant Marine Infrastructure, Safety, and Security, Enhancing Our Rail Safety: Current Challenges for Passenger and Freight Rail, 113th Cong., 2nd sess., March 6, 2014; U.S. Congress, Senate Committee on Appropriations, Subcommittee on Transportation and Housing and Urban Development, and Related Agencies, Rail Safety, 113th Cong., 2nd sess., April 9, 2014.

[72] Platts, *OilGram Price Report,* March 26, 2014, p.1.

[73] "Surge in Rail Shipments of Oil Sidetracks Other Industries; Pileups at BNSF Railway Is Causing Delays for Shippers of Goods Ranging From Coal to Sugar," *The Wall Street Journal*, March 13, 2014.

[74] "Warning: Amtrak Trains Will Not Arrive on Schedule," *Great Falls Tribune,* February 16, 2014.

[75] See, for example, the comments of the CEO of Phillips 66 during the company's earnings conference call, July 31, 2013.

---

### The U.S. Non-contiguous Oil and Gas Trade

The Jones Act is particularly consequential for Puerto Rico, Hawaii, and Alaska. Puerto Rico has no operating refineries. It imports all of its petroleum products. Island countries surrounding Puerto Rico have become major consumers of gasoline and other products refined on the U.S. Gulf Coast, as has the U.S. Virgin Islands, which is not subject to the Jones Act. However, Puerto Rico does not consume any petroleum products of U.S. origin.[76]

Two refineries located near Honolulu supply about 90% of Hawaii's demand for refined products. Most of the crude oil processed in these refineries comes from Indonesia or other Pacific Rim countries; none comes from other parts of the United States.[77] Any oil or refined products shipped from U.S. ports to Hawaii would have to move on Jones Act ships, putting U.S. production at a cost disadvantage against imports from more distant locations.

New drilling technology has also led to a boom in domestic natural gas production. The gas is cooled to minus 260 degrees Fahrenheit for shipment as liquefied natural gas (LNG) aboard special tankers with insulated tanks. There are no Jones Act-qualified LNG tankers available to carry U.S. natural gas to Hawaii and Puerto Rico; the United States has not built an LNG tanker since 1980. In 2011 (P.L. 112-61), Congress allowed three U.S.-built but foreign-flagged LNG tankers to enter the U.S. domestic trade under U.S. flag, but they have not done so; in any event, these vessels were built in the late 1970s and are over 35 years in age. In 1996 (P.L. 104-324), Congress also allowed any foreign-built or foreign-flagged LNG tankers then operating to re-flag under the United States if they would provide service between a U.S. state and Puerto Rico, but none has entered this service. (These vessels would now be at least 18 years old.) Several LNG export terminals are under development in the continental United States, and these could potentially also handle LNG for Puerto Rico and Hawaii. Puerto Rico has an LNG terminal that receives imported gas, mostly from Trinidad and Tobago, and the potential competitiveness of U.S. LNG shipped in Jones Act vessels is uncertain. Hawaii does not have an LNG terminal.

While Alaskan crude oil exports would be required to move in U.S.-flag tankers, the flag requirement does not apply to LNG. Alaska shipped LNG to Japan in foreign-flag tankers until 2012, and such shipments may resume in the future. Alaska gas could be shipped to the U.S. West Coast if Jones Act-qualified LNG tankers were available.[78]

The U.S. Virgin Islands is exempt from the Jones Act.[79] In the 1960s, Hess built what would become the largest refinery in North America (700,000 barrels per day) at St. Croix. The refinery shipped residual fuel oil to the U.S. East Coast (on foreign-flag tankers). It imported crude oil from foreign sources but also received Alaska oil that sailed around Cape Horn in foreign-flag tankers. In 1976, legislation (S. 2422) was introduced to repeal the Jones Act exemption for crude oil and petroleum products, but no action was taken.[80] The refinery closed in February 2012 and is now used as a storage facility while a buyer is being sought.

## Jones Act Waivers

The executive branch has statutory authority to waive the Jones Act "in the interest of national defense."[81] During the summer of 2011, when President Obama released oil from the nation's Strategic Petroleum Reserve (SPR) due to unrest in Libya, the Administration waived the Jones Act and about 25 million barrels of SPR crude oil was moved on foreign-flag tankers to Gulf Coast, East Coast, West Coast, and Hawaii refineries. Each foreign-flag tanker carried 500,000

---

[76] For further information on the Jones Act specific to Puerto Rico, see U.S. Government Accountability Office (GAO), *Puerto Rico: Characteristics of the Island's Maritime Trade and Potential Effects of Modifying the Jones Act*, GAO-13-260, March 2013.

[77] U.S. Energy Information Administration, Geography, U.S. States: http://www.eia.gov/state/?sid=HI.

[78] *Alaska Business Monthly*, "U.S. Cabotage Laws and Alaska's LNG Trade," February 2014.

[79] 46 U.S.C. §55101(b)(4).

[80] U.S. Congress, Senate Committee on Commerce, Subcommittee on Merchant Marine, *Amend the Merchant Marine Act of 1920*, S. 2422, 94th Cong., 2nd sess., February 25, 1976, Serial No. 94-75.

[81] 46 U.S.C. §501.

---

barrels or more in a total of 44 shipments. One delivery was made in a Jones Act vessel, a barge carrying 150,000 barrels.[82]

The Jones Act has also been waived temporarily after disruptions to normal oil supply routes, in the Gulf after Hurricanes Katrina and Rita in 2005, and in the Northeast after superstorm Sandy in 2012. During the 12-day waiver for superstorm Sandy, 12 foreign-flagged tankers transported more than 3 million barrels of refined product from the Gulf Coast to the Northeast.

# Recent U.S. Shipbuilding Activity

Over the past decade, one tank ship and about 125 tank barges have been built in the United States each year, on average. Limited capacity exists in U.S. shipyards to build tankers. As of February 2014, there were 11 petroleum tankers on order for delivery before 2016 and three ATBs on order.[83] Two of these tankers are definitely being built for crude oil, and are planned to replace two Alaska tankers ready for scrapping. The intended use of the other nine ships has not been announced; they could carry either crude or refined products. If they are intended to carry refined products, the shipyard will install coatings on tank walls and more specialized pumping equipment than needed on crude oil tankers, so that the ship can carry a variety of refined products without cross-contamination.

The tanker ships are being built by the General Dynamics NASSCO Shipyard in San Diego and the Aker Philadelphia Shipyard. One industry analysis estimates that NASSCO has the capability of building four large vessels per year and that Aker has the capability of building three, and that these two yards are essentially booked through at least 2016.[84] Recent ATBs have been built by shipyards in Mississippi, Washington, Oregon, and Pennsylvania.

## Foreign Components

NASSCO has partnered with Daewoo Shipbuilding and Aker with Hyundai Mipo Dockyards, both Korean shipbuilders, for ship design, engineering, and procurement support. In the past, shipyard unions have opposed such agreements with Korean shipbuilders because the engines, piping, crew quarters, and portions of the bow and stern were imported from overseas and only assembled in the United States. NASSCO has explained that since Korean yards "build a hundred times more ships, they learn at a rate a hundred times faster, so you learn from the best."[85] Shipyard unions refer to ships built in this manner as "kit ships."[86]

---

[82] Staff memorandum to Members, House Committee on Transportation and Infrastructure, Subcommittee on Coast Guard and Maritime Transportation, regarding hearing, "Review of Vessels Used to Carry Strategic Petroleum Reserve Drawdowns," June 22, 2012.

[83] RBN Energy, LLC, "Rock the Boat Don't Rock the Boat – The Jones Act Articulated Barge Fleet," February 11, 2014.

[84] American Petroleum Tanker Partners LP, Form S-1 Registration Statement, October 22, 2013, p. 114.

[85] Tom Wetherald, General Dynamics NASSCO, panel discussion on U.S. shipbuilding at the Second National Maritime Strategy Symposium, hosted by the Maritime Administration, May 6, 2014; http://www.marad.dot.gov/mariners_landing_page/national_strategy_symposium/National_Maritime_Strategy_Sympo sium.htm.

[86] *Journal of Commerce*, "Unions Sue Over 'Kit' Ships," January 15, 2007; *PR Newswire*, "Metal Trades Department (AFL-CIO) Sues Coast Guard to Block Kit Ships," January 12, 2007.

---

Coast Guard regulations deem a vessel to be U.S. built if (1) all major components of its hull and superstructure are fabricated in the United States, and (2) the vessel is assembled in the United States.[87] The Coast Guard holds that propulsion machinery, other machinery, small engine room equipment modules, consoles, wiring, certain mechanical systems, and outfitting have no bearing on a U.S. build determination.[88]

## Shipbuilding Loans, Grants, and Tax Deferrals

The federal government has long provided financial assistance to domestic shipyards. The so-called "Title XI" program (46 U.S.C. §53702) provides government-backed loan guarantees (with repayment over 25 years) for prospective buyers of U.S.-built vessels as well as to shipyards for modernization of their facilities. The loan guarantee covers 87.5% of the cost of a ship. In FY2014, Congress appropriated $38 million for the program, the first time it has provided funds to expand the loan portfolio in several years. For FY2015, the House passed bill (H.R. 4745) would rescind $29 million of this amount while the Senate reported bill (S. 2438) provides $7 million for the program. For each loan, a reserve amount must be held depending on the risk, but typically 5% to 10% of the loan amount. As of April 2014, MARAD had $73 million available for new guarantees, enough to cover approximately $735 million of loans and a current portfolio of outstanding loan guarantees totaling $1.7 billion covering about 250 vessels.[89]

The Title XI program has been controversial in Congress when large loan recipients have defaulted, like in October 2001, when American Classic Voyages defaulted on a loan for two cruise ships intended for the Hawaii trade. Other borrowers have defaulted since.[90] Foreign yards are subsidized also, although the form of assistance is often not transparent. An international agreement to reduce shipbuilding subsidies failed largely because the six largest U.S. shipyards objected to reducing the Title XI program.[91]

In the National Defense Authorization Act for FY2006 (P.L. 109-163, §3506), Congress created a grant program for small shipyards (currently defined as having no more than 1,200 employees). The grant can cover up to 75% of the cost of improving their facilities. Since then, about $10-$15 million a year has been made available for this program, except that the American Recovery and Reinvestment Act of 2009 provided $100 million and no funds were appropriated in FY2014.

---

[87] 49 C.F.R. §67.97.

[88] The Philadelphia Metal Trades Council sued the Coast Guard, but a U.S. District Court sided with the Coast Guard. See *Philadelphia Metal Trades Council v. Allen*, No. 07-145 (E.D. Pa. Jan. 12, 2007).

[89] MARAD, FY2015 Budget Request.

[90] Information on defaults is not available on MARAD's Title XI homepage. On July 14, 2010, the Maritime Administrator at the time testified that since 1993, there had been 13 defaults including two in FY2009 and two in FY2010. Testimony of David Matsuda, House Armed Services Committee on Seapower and Expeditionary Forces, Hearing on Activities of the Maritime Administration, July 14, 2010.

[91] After nearly a decade of receiving no shipbuilding subsidies in the 1980s, U.S. shipyards urged the government to negotiate an international agreement. In 1993, Congress resumed funding for Title XI. In 1994, after five years of negotiations, the United States, the European Union, Norway, Japan, and South Korea reached an agreement through the Organization for Economic Cooperation and Development to prohibit most shipbuilding subsidies. The United States would have been required to reduce Title XI guarantees to 80% of the loan amount and to limit them to 12 years. The so-called "big six" shipyards that do mostly Navy work, but some commercial work, objected to the agreement. The U.S. yards that do mostly commercial work supported it. The United States was the only participant that did not ratify the agreement.

MARAD also administers the Capital Construction Fund (CCF) program, which allows U.S.-flag operators to defer taxes on income placed in such a fund if used to purchase or reconstruct U.S. built ships.[92] The fund is established by the ship owner subject to MARAD regulations and reporting requirements.[93] The investment income in the CCF is also tax deferred. The tax deferral is essentially indefinite as long as the program remains active.

# U.S.-flag Reservation for Export of Oil and Natural Gas?

Congress is debating whether to allow crude oil produced in the continental United States to be exported to other countries, in addition to Canada.[94] Domestic producers of natural gas are seeking federal export permits.[95] Current law would not require that such exports be carried in U.S.-flagged ships.[96] Many U.S.-based petroleum producers and refiners control foreign-flag tankers, some of which deliver imported crude oil to the United States or export refined petroleum products from U.S. refineries. U.S. merchant mariners are seeking additional U.S.-flag voyages because the government-impelled cargos (military and food-aid cargos) they rely on are in decline.

During markup of the Coast Guard and Maritime Transportation Act of 2014 (H.R. 4005) an amendment to require that LNG exports move in U.S.-crewed and eventually in U.S.-built tankers was withdrawn in favor of a Government Accountability Office study of maritime employment related to this requirement.[97] Also unsuccessful were two amendments to a House-passed energy bill (H.R. 6, passed on June 25, 2014) which sought to require that LNG exports be carried in U.S.-flag tankers and require that federal regulators give priority to export terminal projects that would use U.S.-flag vessels.[98] Amendments to the Energy and Water Appropriations Act of 2015 (H.R. 4923) would have tied federal approval of LNG export terminals to the use of U.S.-flag tankers, but they were defeated on points of order.[99]

Whether the nation's energy trade should be carried in U.S.-flag tankers is a long-standing debate in Congress. In 2006, when the United States was still expected to be an importer rather than an exporter of LNG, Congress specified that federal regulators give "top priority" to the processing of licenses for offshore LNG import terminals if they would be supplied by U.S.-flag tankers, so as to promote the security of the United States.[100] LNG shippers contended that tying U.S. trade

---

[92] 46 U.S.C. §53501.

[93] 46 C.F.R. Parts 390 and 391.

[94] CRS Report R43442, *U.S. Crude Oil Export Policy: Background and Considerations*, by Phillip Brown et al.

[95] CRS Report R42074, *U.S. Natural Gas Exports: New Opportunities, Uncertain Outcomes*, by Michael Ratner et al.

[96] U.S. law (The Cargo Preference Act) requires 50% of "U.S. government impelled" cargo, such as food-aid, to be shipped in U.S.-flag ships, but these do not have to be U.S. built. Most of these ships also receive operating subsidies because they are to be made available to the military as part of the Maritime Security Fleet program.

[97] H.Rept. 113-384, Howard Coble Coast Guard and Maritime Transportation Act of 2014, p. 27.

[98] *Congressional Record*, June 25, 2014, p. H5750.

[99] H.Amdt. 1029 and H.Amdt. 1031 to H.R. 4923.

[100] P.L. 109-241, §304.

---

routes to certain flag vessels would hinder the ability to supply LNG under short-term contracts, which was how LNG was increasingly traded as the global market matured.[101]

Security was the rationale put forth by proponents of requiring U.S. imported oil to be carried in U.S.-flag tankers in the 1970s. In 1974, The Energy Transportation Security Act (ETSA, H.R. 8193, 93rd Congress) would have required that 30% of imported oil be carried in U.S.-flag and U.S. built tankers. The bill was pocket-vetoed by President Ford. In the 94th Congress (1975), Congress created the Strategic Petroleum Reserve in response to the supply crisis in imported oil (P.L. 94-163). Since the oil for the reserve is purchased by the federal government, half the oil shipped by vessel must be transported by U.S.-flag tankers pursuant to the Cargo Preference Act of 1954.[102] In the 95th Congress (1977), the ETSA was reintroduced (H.R. 1037, S. 61) with modifications. A version requiring that 9.5% of U.S. imported oil be carried in U.S.-flag tankers passed the House by voice vote, but was then defeated in a recorded vote of 257 to 165. In the House floor debate, supporters of the bill primarily cited national security and the importance of boosting the domestic shipbuilding base.[103] While opponents cited costs to consumers and potential retaliation from trading partners, much of their argument reflected a Common Cause report on political campaign contributions by the U.S.-flag industry, which had been released just days before.[104] That neither the Department of Defense nor Department of State had testified in support of a national security rationale for the bill was also noted in the floor debate. The Senate never took up the measure.

At a 2014 industry symposium organized by MARAD to solicit ideas for addressing the decline in U.S.-flag cargoes, several participants advocated requiring a certain amount of LNG exports be carried in U.S.-flag or U.S.-built ships.[105] Much of the discussion concerned additional statutory or regulatory requirements for staying the decline in cargoes. There was little or no discussion, given the inverse relationship between price and quantity demanded, of efficiencies that could lower the price of U.S.-flag shipping.[106] The one commercial shipper making a presentation at the symposium stated, "Today U.S. flag is seen as a group of carriers that we have to use. I think that going forward, to be successful, you have to be seen as a group of carriers that we want to use."[107]

---

[101] See filings of Shell and the Center for LNG at http://www.regulations.gov under docket no. MARAD-2007-26841.

[102] At the time, the GAO estimated that U.S.-flag shipping costs would be 2.3 to 2.8 times that of foreign-flag rates and questioned whether there was an adequate supply of U.S.-flag tankers. GAO, *Transportation Planning For The Strategic Petroleum Reserve Should Be Improved*, LCD-78-211, October 18, 1978.

[103] *Congressional Record – House*, October 19, 1977, p. 34177 et seq.

[104] "The Maritime Payoff," *Wall Street Journal*, August 4, 1977; "The Great Ship Robbery," *New York Times*, August 6, 1977; "How To Buy A Bill," *The Washington Post*, September 1, 1977.

[105] For webcasts, transcripts and presentations at the symposium, see http://www.marad.dot.gov/mariners_landing_page/national_strategy_symposium/National_Maritime_Strategy_Sympo sium.htm.

[106] This focus is consistent with the observation of a former Maritime Administrator that the U.S. merchant marine has "become accustomed to thinking that the government could never do enough for them." Andrew Gibson and Arthur Donovan, *The Abandoned Ocean* (Columbia, SC: Univ. of South Carolina Press, 2000), p. 175.

[107] Scott Mogavero, Global Logistics and Planning Manager at GE Logistics, as quoted in *Journal of Commerce*, "Shippers Cite U.S.-Flag Challenges," January 15, 2014.

# Current Legislation

Several bills now pending in Congress address matters related to waterborne transportation of oil, including many of the safety and commercial issues raised in this report:

The Coast Guard and Maritime Transportation Act of 2014 (H.R. 4005, passed by the House April 1, 2014) directs the U.S. Department of Transportation to submit a national maritime strategy that identifies federal regulations that reduce the competitiveness of U.S.-flag vessels in international trade, submit recommendations to make U.S.-flag vessels more competitive and enhance U.S. shipbuilding capability, and identify strategies to increase the use of U.S.-flag vessels to carry imports and exports and domestic commerce. The Coast Guard is directed to arrange with the National Academy of Sciences an assessment of laws that impact the ability of U.S.-flag vessels to compete in international trade, while GAO is directed to study how U.S. maritime employment would be affected by a requirement that LNG exports move in U.S.-flag vessels.

S. 2444, the Coast Guard Authorization Act for Fiscal Years 2015 and 2016, would require the Coast Guard to report marine casualties to state or tribal governments within 24 hours, publish on a publicly accessible website its incident action plans in response to an oil spill, and modify oil spill contingency plans to include advance planning for closing and reopening of fishing grounds.

H.R. 2838, sponsored by Resident Commissioner Pierluisi, would exempt liquefied natural gas and propane tankers serving Puerto Rico from the Jones Act. S. 1483, sponsored by Senator Cantwell, establishes a federal oil spill research committee and requires updates to vessel oil spill response plans.

The National Defense Authorization Act for FY2015 (H.R. 4435), as passed by the House on May 22, 2014, declares the sense of Congress (§3503) that "the United States coastwise trade laws [the Jones Act] promote a strong domestic trade maritime industry, which supports the national security and economic vitality of the United States and the efficient operation of the United States transportation system."

## Author Contact Information

John Frittelli
Specialist in Transportation Policy
jfrittelli@crs.loc.gov, 7-7033

## Acknowledgments

James C. Uzel, GIS Analyst, and Amber Hope Wilhelm, Graphics Specialist, contributed to the figures in this report.

www.ingramcontent.com/pod-product-compliance
Lightning Source LLC
Chambersburg PA
CBHW080755290526
45790CB00008B/3449